NATIONAL
GEOGRAPHIC

The Night Sky

Felix James

At night I look out my window.
I look up at the sky.
The sky is dark, but I can still see some things.

In the morning I look out
my window.
I can't see the stars
and moon,
but they are there.
I will see them tonight.

12

I see the moon.
The moon is big
and round.

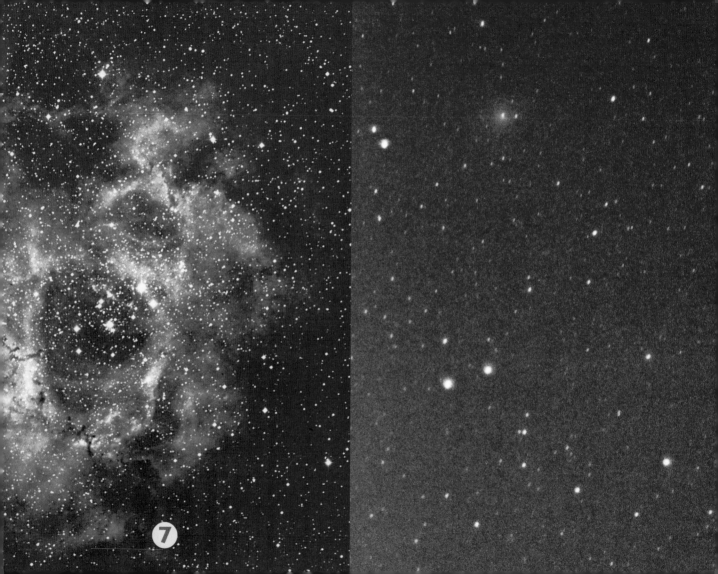

I see stars.
There are a lot of stars
in the night sky.
Stars look like tiny dots
of light.
They look tiny
because they are far away.

3